the
autobiography
of a
jukebox

Books by Cornelius Eady:

Kartunes
Victims of the Latest Dance Craze
Boom, Boom, Boom: A Chapbook
The Gathering of My Name
You Don't Miss Your Water
The Autobiography of a Jukebox

the
autobiography
of a
jukebox

poems by
cornelius eady

Carnegie Mellon University Press
Pittsburgh 1997

Acknowledgments

Some of the poems in this collection have appeared, at times in different forms, in the following periodicals:

Ackee: "Leavin' Trunk"
Callaloo: "The Cab Driver Who Ripped Me Off"
Colorado Review: "Johnny on the Mainline"
Drumvoices Review: "Youngblood", "Hard Times"
Kenyon Review: "Photo of Miles Davis at Lennies-on-the-Turnpike, 1968"
Muleteeth: "The House", "Tramp"
Pennsylvania Review: "Chuck Berry"
Phoebe: "Photo of a Max Roach Solo, 1964"
Prairie Schooner: "Anger", "A Small Moment", "Photo of Dexter Gordon, About to Solo, 1965"
River Styx: "Why Was I Born? A Duet between John Coltrane and Kenny Burrell"
Red Brick Review: "Walt Whitman Mall", "The Death of Sam Patch"
Seneca Review: "I'm a Fool to Love You" (then titled "Empty Choice Blues"), "My Mother's Blues About the Numbers"
The William and Mary Review: "Charlie Chaplin Impersonates a Poet"

"King Snake" first appeared in *Eternal Light: Poems About Grandparents*, edited by Jason Shinder, Harcourt Brace.

The quote by Larry Neal is from his book *Hoodoo Hollerin' Bebop Ghosts*, Howard University Press

I would like to thank the John Simon Guggenheim Memorial Foundation and The Writers' Room, Inc. for providing me the time and space to work on this book. I would also like to thank the Rockefeller Foundation for its generous Fellowship to its Study and Conference Center in Bellagio, Italy. Finally, thanks to Sarah Micklem, Toi Derricotte, Shreela Ray, Marian Woods, Jason Shinder, Shelley Messing and Julie Bruck for reading and suggestions.

Publication of this book is supported by grants from the National Endowment for the Arts in Washington, D.C., a Federal agency, and from the Pennsylvania Council on the Arts.

Library of Congress Catalog Card Number: 94-68937
ISBN: 0-88748-211-2
ISBN: 0-88748-212-0 Pbk.

10 9 8 7 6 5 4 3 2 1

This book is for Gloria, Roosevelt and Marie Eady

Contents

1: **Home Front**

2: **Rodney King Blues**

3: **The Bruise of the Lyric**

4: **Small Moments**

And check this: lurking between odd pages in a book
of blues, your handwriting in red ink . . .
—Larry Neal

1: Home Front

I'm a Fool to Love You

Some folks will tell you the blues is a woman,
Some type of supernatural creature.
My mother would tell you, if she could,
About her life with my father,
A strange and sometimes cruel gentleman.
She would tell you about the choices
A young black woman faces.
Is falling in with some man
A deal with the devil
In blue terms, the tongue we use
When we don't want nuance
To get in the way,
When we need to talk straight?
My mother chooses my father
After choosing a man
Who was, as we sing it,
Of no account.
This man made my father look good,
That's how bad it was.
He made my father seem like an island
In the middle of a stormy sea,
He made my father look like a rock.
And is the blues the moment you realize
You exist in a stacked deck,
You look in a mirror at your young face,
The face my sister carries,
And you know it's the only leverage
You've got?
Does this create a hurt that whispers
How you going to do?
Is the blues the moment
You shrug your shoulders
And agree, a girl without money
Is nothing, dust

To be pushed around by any old breeze?
Compared to this,
My father seems, briefly,
To be a fire escape.
This is the way the blues works
Its sorry wonders,
Makes trouble look like
A feather bed,
Makes the wrong man's kisses
A healing.

Money Won't Change It (but time will take you on)

You're rich, lady, hissed the young woman at
My mother as she bent in her garden.
Look at what you've got, and it was
Too much, the collards and tomatoes,
A man, however lousy, taking care
of the bills.

This was the reason for the early deaths
My mother was to find from that point on,
Turned dirt and the mock of roots,
Until finally, she gave her garden up.
You can't have nothing, she tells us,
Is the motto of our neighborhood,
These modest houses
That won't give an inch.

Who Wrote the Book of Love?

My mother has been at work
For years on a book
She wants published, but won't
Show to anyone.
Sometimes I think that's what
It must be about, as sheaf after
Sheaf of notebook paper is
Requested, bought, and disappears.
Sometimes I think
I understand her habit:
This is the way I learned to write
In that house, on a cot in a small, blue room.
This is her book to and about Jesus,
Who blows love in her poor ear.
Jesus, the man my daddy once saw
Lying next to her
On her old army cot.
Tender son of God,
Saint of the neglected housewife,
My father sees this,
And jumps from the house,
Impressed, but unchanged.

When Jesus returns
As she believes he will,
Or she to him,
Will her reward
Be the greater for this,
These penciled stories
She has witnessed
And outlasted?
Will her spirit house be grander,
Furnished with everything

She couldn't win or hold on to
In this life?

I already regret the day
I'll find it,
(Too late, Lord),
Bunched under
Her mattress, an aleph
Jumbled like rare but corroded
Half dollars.

My Mother's Blues About the Numbers

My mother didn't get to keep
Much in her life. She tells me this story
Of the one time she hit big
On the numbers,
Guessed it, and hit it,
And then somehow lost it all
To my father and cousin.
Perhaps she trusted my father
Once too often,
And allowed him to pick up
Her winnings.
Maybe she fell asleep
A winner,
And woke up
To an empty wound
Of a hiding place,
A dream of greedy,
Prying hands
That wasn't a dream,
A crime too soft
To wake her up.

She's waited for years
For them to own up.
They'd laugh that laugh
That says: *A woman*
Can't prove nothin'.
My father's dead.
She's waiting now
For my cousin
To come forward,

But a man will never
Lift a woman

Towards the truth.
That's what these blues say,
That a woman must carry
To her moldering ground.

The Yankee Dollar

My sister has a prayer:
Please lord, let me have my money now,
You know it won't do me any good
When I'm gone.

25 thousand dollars *cash   money*
Is what my mother is waiting for
Before she'll move out of
The calamity we call my dead father's house.
A fee, her brain tells her,
She deserves for writing her book.
Nothing less will salve the wound
She called living with my father,
And nothing I can offer will change it.
A son's money is a man's money,
And a man's money, no matter how friendly it's offered
WIll get in your business, sooner or later.
This is what a woman looks like
When she'd had enough, I think,
The hardness which squeezes her eyes
Into hard points, the way the mouth
Curves its scorn,
This is what the blues looks like
When it creeps into a small chamber of the heart
And like a weevil, decides it's found a home.
I want my own, she says,
A key and a lock,
A deed with her ink on the line,
And the men she carries in her head,
Sometimes my father, now sometimes me,
To bow our heads and step aside.

The House

In my old neighborhood,
The house my father bought
With my aunt is still standing,
But it's a pitiful thing.
My father had nurtured a reputation
As a minor money bag,
So it's small wonder
He got hit up by contractors
Who needed to give him
The homeowner's blues:
Cheatin' pipes,
Wires that double-crossed,
Laughed when they
Threw you down.

By then he was
A pensioner,
Who would spend his days
Asleep in his Cadillac
To escape his wife,
A woman who would
Glower at him
Through the living room window,
Wondering when he
Was going to give
Her life back.

Why would a man
Who had always measured his charity
Fall for so many hustles?
Inside
The walls were plastered
With half-truths,
Fast-talk,

The old switcheroo,
And you wondered
What crazy heaven
They had promised
On easy terms?

What am I supposed to do with
This mess, this legacy?
I wanted to know,
After we returned
From his service.
A house in a town
I've done my level best
To leave,

His unmarried widow
Left flat broke.

And the blues rolled up
In a moving van,
Found itself
Sanctuary.

Hesitation Blues

I am five or six years old, and my mother is on her knees. She is at the county welfare office, and something has gone wrong. The assistance she'd hoped for isn't going to happen, and she is at the end of her rope.

She has three children, and whatever our daddy is doing, it either isn't enough, or it's barely too much, since her arguments will not move whomever is sitting behind this desk, looking at the top of her head.

My mother has fallen for love, for mercy, for her children, to her knees.

But there will be no pity for whatever sorrows have pushed her to this. To the ears I can't fully remember, her crisis must have rung of back door blues. How impatient they must have become for my mother to rise, O careless love, O easy rider, off their hard luck floor.

Leavin' Trunk

He's sitting in a car, watching my sister's house, the man
who's trying to dog my sister down. Old, and toothless, he's
the man who helps her to pay her bills.

And my sister's sick of it, sick and tired of living the way
she does, and she's beginning to wonder if there isn't
something better she can do with the rest of her life. She's
in her early 40's. She's beginning to think about moving
back home.

She's tired of Mr. Pitiful, who wants too much for his
bottom dollar. He watches the house. He spooks her steps.
His face is at her bedroom window.

My sister's dreaming of making a midnight creep, of leaving
him, a sucker with a mule to ride. She wants the rails to
sing of her getaway, no traces left when he pushes open her
front door.

And though it'll turn out she's only trading one bad man for
another, for my father, who keeps on ice the file of all the
things she ought to have done right, in her mind she closes
the books, packs her trunk, to see if there's any way in this
life to earn a dollar a man can't touch.

I Want to Fly Like Superman

Marie, my niece, is standing on the roof of my cousin's garage.

This is a game. My cousin's children are on the ground, taunting her to jump.

This isn't a game. Her mother has left her to live in Florida. Her grandmother, who tried, is too confused to take her on. My father pays my cousin for her room and board. *Watch your step*, she hears on her first night there, *don't you know you're here 'cause they don't want you?*

Maybe she dreams of this as she teeters. Perhaps she believes it's possible for the wind to read her desires, scoop out her body like a wing, lift her so they might finally see, illuminated in their disbelief, her true worth.

Instead, she hits the pavement. Instead, as she'll tell me and my wife years after the fact, she will lie there and bleed and listen to their jokes and wait for a neighbor to happen by to help her. She will learn that the main rule of this family is: there is no obligation to save a fool.

Johnny on the Mainline

Small prayers must have been invented for people like my cousin Johnny, whom I have decided to drive, partly for old times, partly to get him away from my Mother's house, to where he'd like to go in my rental car.

This man, who I am quickly learning I don't know well at all anymore, is a broken heart, and a heartbreaker. My sister tells me somehow out of earshot before we leave, that he's a big time crackhead. He scares her.

He scares my sister, who always packs a gun and knife, is what I'm thinking, as the neighborhood streets grow leaner, and he asks me to pull up in front of what can't be anything else but the house where he gets his stuff.

Some buddies of his are in front of the place, drinking half–pints of beer. They wave at him, look hard at me.

We both know what should happen next, but instead of turning me into a real humorous story for the cops, he only hits me up for a small levy.

"You're family" he says before he takes my change, and this will be enough, this time, to let me off easy, though his hunger smells a tourist.

Santa Claus (come straight to the ghetto)

It is Christmas Eve, and my good sense won't speak to me.
A woman has flagged me down to beg for money for food,
and I have stopped at night in my old neighborhood and
rolled down the electric window of my rental car.

It is the night before Christmas, and I refuse to listen to the
obvious. The doors are power-locked, the engine is in gear
and running. Though it is snowing I have clear visibility in
the mirror. I decide I can handle this.

And had I been wrong that night, had a gun suddenly
appeared from under her coat, had a friend moved from a
blindspot into my face, who in the world would have
understood? Not the cops, not my family and friends, not
my wife, set agrieving by a whim. Not a soul could have
answered *why the hell did he stop?*

Nothing happens, but I have made a mistake. This is not
compassion as she rolls down her sleeve in answer to a
question I never ask; as she takes my idiot money and runs
as fast as she can away from my car and the shops on Main
Street, towards everything I have given her.

Almost Grown

My father loves my sister so much, he has to strike her. He cares for her so deeply that he has crossed, for the first and only time, into my mother's domain.

He has caught his daughter red-handed at the front door, trying to sneak home late from her boyfriend's house.

And my father, poor ghost, knows too much. Without ever leaving the house, he has overheard every sweet thing this man, an old buddy of his, has whispered to her in bed.

Tonight, my sister discovers her only power. As she tussles with him on the front porch, she is all heat and righteous passion.

He will never try this hard again to tell anyone how much he loves them. With his belt, my father tries to tell my sister what he knows a man is capable of, but all he does is tell her fortune.

Too Young to Know

One day my father chopped down
The old apricot tree
Which used to live in my parents' backyard.
My father deflected my anger at him
With a look I heard Muddy Waters sing:
Ya'll too young to know.

When I went to my mother
For the truth,
I heard only
What he must have told her:
A vague story about roots
   and basement pipes,
A vague story about branches
   and kitchen windows
Punctuated by a shrug which meant:
He just does what he does.

The blues don't know nothing about trees,
Unless, of course,
It's enlisted the moon
To drag some shadows around,
Unless, of course,
Something jumps up
Out of a hollow log,
A worry you didn't need
To cross your path.

My father's gone,
The tree's a stump,
And I'm still too young to know
If one day I'll glance
   out my window
At the sycamore
And cluck my teeth.

Them That Got

At my father's memorial service, one of the many cousins I've never met before this moment is telling us a story of how my father once helped him out.

It seems when my cousin was younger, he needed some cash in order to start a business. He goes to my father to ask for a loan.

"Unk," (my father's nickname outside the immediate family), "it's bound to work. All I need is the start–up money."

My father thought about it, my cousin tells us, and then he asks, "Have you been to the bank?"

"Yes," my cousin tells him.

"They give you any money?" my father asks.

"No."

"If the bank didn't give you any money," says my daddy, "why should I?"

This cousin was wounded for years by my father's reply, but now, he tells us, he understands what my father was really trying to tell him, that he could only rely on himself, that if you want something bad enough, you have to go out there and get it.

But it wasn't God Bless the Child he was singing, I thought to myself as I saw my daddy keep his hands in his deep, deep pockets, as I listened to my cousin, who never got his business, try his Christian best to turn a skinflint into a reasonable man.

I'm Walkin'

This was how my daddy would threaten my mother when he felt she was becoming too much of a trial:

O, one day, he'd tell her, he would just pack up and move back to the small town in Florida where he came from.

He still had people there. He'd get a smaller house, something he could handle.

His people would take care of what he couldn't.

Maybe he would fish. Certainly, he'd be left alone.

Certainly, he'd get to spend his final days in peace.

And he'd get a look on his face as if he believed there was a domestic God that sprinkled mercy on a husband's complaints.

My mama would cackle.

'Buked and Scorned

Even if I had asked, I don't believe I could have ever been made to understand the blues my father must have felt the evening he opened the door to our house only to find that his wife and daughter had temporarily quit him, packed their bags and moved like a whisper down the road.

How did it feel for him to move from room to room of a world he knew he had owned that morning?

Of course his women had left the household a mocking mess; of course every house on the street had felt the corrosive wake of their leaving as the victory taxi pushed off from the curb.

What kind of world did the blues show my daddy that night, as he walked alone through the dust of their threats, through the accusations he thought they were only kidding him about?

I Don't Want Nobody to Give Me Nothing (open up the door, I'll get it myself)

I never asked my father if he had ever felt racism on his job.

He never liked to talk about it, but once he mentioned what happened at work a few days after he moved from the manhole to behind the wheel of the truck, a plum of a job he'd earned fair and square through union seniority.

A white guy assigned to his truck began to give him grief, and it became clear real fast that he wasn't going to let up.

My daddy was still a large man. One of my cousins who grew up with him told me of my father's crazy days in the small Florida town they'd grown up in. The Eady Brothers were known as holy terrors, niggers who went looking for fights. Citizens took them for real.

But this, of course, was a different struggle, in its way slightly more dangerous than a barroom. My daddy got what he came up to the north to get, and it's at the end of a long work day that he gets the white man alone in his cab, and tells him in a quiet voice, *look, buddy. I know you don't like this, but you're doing your job, and I'm doing mine.*

It shouldn't work, but it does. Lord knows, my daddy could be a difficult man, but in moments like these, he was Darwin's angel. That was how he kept money in his pockets. That was why he was allowed to die a natural death.

King Snake

Sometimes, my father's young life would resemble
something you'd hear in a Muddy Waters song.

Like the time he found out that the local hospitals would
pay good money for rattlesnakes in order to make anti-
venom.

Soon he had a pen full, and I want to imagine my non-
body, his yet-to-be, whispering *careful* in his ear as he seeks
out his dangerous two bits, but he's young, and reckless,
and I know how he gets when he sees a way to grab a buck.

I suppose his name gets around West Florida, because one
day a white man drives up to the house and makes a better
offer: One dollar a snake.

Of course he takes it, but when the white man who was
only paying my father fifty cents shows up, he doesn't take
kindly to the new arrangement. He curses my daddy out,
and threatens to return with the law.

This is a story my father thinks is no big deal, really, just
the daily stuff he had to do to live down there, and I can
see he's wondering why I want to make something of it.

But when the white man comes back, hauling with him the
sheriff, he gives me a description of my grandfather, a black
man with a long, handle-bar mustache, who owns his land
and holds a certain reputation.

When angered, we both stammer; unlike me, no one cares
to get him to that point.

This is proven by the way my father says the sheriff decides to handle the situation.

When the car pulls up, my grandfather stands in the front door. Tall? Stout? With Indian blood? No matter; he's a quiet black man, on his own land, in the south in the late twenties or early thirties, holding a shotgun. Holding a shotgun and saying nothing else.

My father can never tell me what my grandfather did to earn this moment, what crazy, selfless or fearful things came before that would lead the sheriff to side against the wounded pride of a white southern man.

And I want to yell, as wind blowing dust across the front yard, *watch your step* into their ears, but they both know more than I do, that nothing's going to happen, that they're all going to let the poor, silly man yell until his face turns red, and he simply runs out of breath and insults. My daddy will never be able to tell me what it was about my grandfather that tells the sheriff this just ain't worth the dance, or what it is in my sister that recalls my granddad to the relatives who knew him.

When my daddy was a young boy, he played with rattlesnakes. Can't you just hear Muddy Waters and Little Walter juking that out?

So baby, I sure know how to handle you.

2: Rodney King Blues

The Cab Driver Who Ripped Me Off

That's right, said the cab driver,
Turning the corner to the
Round-a-bout way,
Those stupid, fuckin' beggars,
You know the guys who
Walk up to my cab
With their hands extended
And their little cups?
You know their problem?
You know what's wrong with them?
They ain't got no brains.
I mean, they don't know nothin'
'cause if they had brains
They'd think of a way
To find a job.
You know what one of 'em told me once?
He said what he did,
Begging
He said it was work.
Begging
Was work.
And I told him
Straight to his face:
That ain't work.
You think that's work?
Let me tell you what work is:
Work is something that you do
That's of value
To someone else.
Now you take me.
It takes brains to do
What I do.
You know what I think?
I think they ought to send

All these beggars over
To some other country,
Any country,
It don't matter which,
For 3, 4, years,
Let them wander around
Some other country,
See how they like that.
We ought to make a
National program
Sending them off
To wander about
Some other country
For a few years,
Let 'em beg over there,
See how far it gets them.
I mean, look at that guy
You know, who was big
In the sixties,
That drug guy,
Timothy Leary?
Yeah, he went underground,
Lived overseas.
You know what?
A few years abroad
And he was ready to
Come back
On any terms.
He didn't care if
They arrested him.
He said
The U.S. is better
Than any country

In the world.
Send them over there
For a few years.
They'd be just like him.
This is the greatest country
In the whole world.
Timothy Leary
Was damn happy
To get back here,
And he's doing fine.
Look at me.
I used to be like that.
I used to live underground.
I came back.
I think all those beggars got
  a mental block.
I think you should do something.
I mean, you ought to like
  what you do,
But you should do something.
Something of use
To the community.
All those people,
Those bums,
Those scam artists,
Those hustlers,
Those drug addicts,
Those welfare cheats,
Those sponges.
Other than that
I don't hold nothin'
Against no one.
Hey, I picked you up.

Rodney King Blues

I love the world,
But my heart's
Been cheated.

What's in my hands?
Pain, a low
Moan. That's

What it feels like.
Now every street
Shadows my steps.
A sin
And a shame.

What do I carry?
There's
Mr. Death

In his severe
Blue uniform,
Mr. Misfortune
And his legal fists.
A low–
Down funk.

What's on my heart?
'Buke
And scorn,
Mr. Hard Luck's
Satisfaction.

Blue musk.
Sorrowful shoes.
Rodney King Blues.

Anger

I am trying to calm down. Again. I am forcing myself to think of the plants in my wife's garden. I am trying to avoid confrontation. I am living in fear of nuance.

It has been a very difficult few weeks, these days after the verdict and the LA riots. Last night, after watching some spin doctors do their stuff, I reached for my pen. I was going to write a letter to the op ed page when I stopped and thought about it.

It would be difficult to stuff my anger into an envelope, harder still, even dangerous, to send it through the US Postal System.

I have an anger that could, as they say, lay waste to planets. I have an anger that could only converse with volcanoes. It is surly and diffident and doesn't care to talk about it.

O, haughty anger, O dark sunglassed angel repository, O unreasonable man, all that would spill onto the mail room floor would amount to an inarticulate sputter. That's what I told myself, but now as I sit in the back yard, dark beer in my hand, a sun shining on flowers I would have called normal last month, I hear a voice.

What Is Hip?

It was most likely my tie which set off the suspicion, a hand-painted one made by my sister-in-law, based on African prints. Normally, it's enough of a culture passport, but tonight, in this lower east side art space, it seems to spell BUPPIE. I mean, would any righteous dude be caught dead wearing any tie down there on a Saturday night?

For myself, the answer seemed easy, but when the writer whose reading I'd come down here for gently teases *What's up with you? You look so normal.* And I catch the rapid once–over from The Brother With The Dreads as he walks up to us, beginning with my red hightops, and ending with the partial fade in my hair, which causes my writer friend to jump to my defense with, *The Brother teaches college,*

I thought of the story of June Jordan's high heels clacking A SISTER'S HERE in the white halls of Barnard College,

And that poor black entrepreneur, a gentleman not much older than my father was, his store burnt out by his own community during the riots in LA, shouting to a group of young bloods standing across the street, WHAT THE HELL'S WRONG WITH YOU? COULDN'T YOU SEE I WAS MAKING IT? COULDN'T YOU SEE I WAS DOING IN A WHITE MAN'S WORLD?

The Killing Floor

It just isn't fair, I read and watch and hear after the tit-for-tat incident after the verdict in LA, the poor white man who was dragged out of the cab of his truck and beaten nearly to death as the cameras whirled above in a traffic helicopter.

It isn't easy to watch the little dance a kid in shorts gives as he gets his boots in. He's a tiny rumba of death, long-legged and gangly in the way only a teen can move, he's the shadow of a crazed stork.

And O, strange mirror, how quickly they took the hint, as they recite the jury's translation:

Is this what you mean? ask their boots and clubs, ask their arms which have plucked a stranger into helplessness, *Anytime? Anyplace? Just because?*

Nobody's Fault But Mine

On TV, a cop is trying to explain to us what is actually occurring in the Rodney King videotape.

Don't believe your eyes, he's telling the host. He claims it's all Rodney's fault, that Rodney actually controls the event by not staying down.

This is the theory the jury bought, and this cop is on the air to give us a blow-by-blow rationalization.

His main point being, Rodney didn't seem to understand the drill. He kept trying to rise and get away, and at one point the officer stops the tape to let us all in on a small revelation.

By then, I have forced myself to stop counting the number of times poor Rodney King's body has informed his lizard brain that he's in big trouble, mortal danger, that it's night, that he's alone, surrounded and being beaten by cops screaming proof that his ass is theirs, is grass, that there will be no other witnesses besides the police.

Which blow convinces him that this is his death, come tripping on the run, death raining down hard as blues upon his amazed skull.

How many times does Rodney King's wrecked body scream at him, *this is for real, you'd better get up and run for your life,* until his injuries take on a kind of dumb luck, he finally becomes too hurt to move, just at the moment the cop freezes the action, informs us that had Rodney risen one time more, they would have been forced to draw their weapons, take off the kid gloves.

Dread

I'm going to tell you something
It's a simple fact of life.
If you're a young man in East New York,
Here's a simple fact of life:
If they don't shoot you with a gun,
They'll cut you with a knife.

I'm standing at the grave
Of a just-buried friend,
Staring at the fresh mound
Of a just-buried friend.
Don't know how it got started,
Can't see where it'll end.

Looked for a glass of water
But they gave me turpentine
You can ask for a glass of water
All you'll get is turpentine
I don't know why this life
Is like askin' a brick for wine.

I've lost eight friends already,
Who'll make number nine?
Lord, buried eight friends already,
Who'll be number nine?
I'd love to make plans with you, Sugar,
But I don't believe we'll have the time.

I sleep with the bullet
That didn't have my name,
Say *good morning* to the bullet
That didn't have my name,
So when my number comes up, baby,
It'll be the one thing you can't blame.

3: The Bruise of the Lyric

Why Was I Born? A Duet Between John Coltrane & Kenny Burrell

So why? Asks the guitar(ist),
And the sax(ophonist),
A genius, a lover,
Side-steps the question,
Blows a kiss instead.
Then they both begin to speak
Like bourbon being poured
Into a glass at
Which bar? The eternal one
Bathed in the open light
Of the test pattern, the one
Where the phone booths
Are all functional, but
So? Better here than
Your shitty apartment,
His/Her scent on the
Bed sheets until wash day,
Perhaps longer. Better here
Than finding lipstick
On a bathroom glass, his
Brand of cigarette on the dresser.
Their melody is the touch you now wish
You'd never learned, the caress
Of fingers and breath
That promised, promised. What
Hurts is beautiful, the bruise
Of the lyric.

Photo of a Max Roach Solo, 1964

The photo attempts to explain, in its way,
The great, beautiful dark we refer to as
A jazz club. In the center
Of its frame, the blurred forearm
Of the modern jazz drummer,
A kind pioneer in a leisure suit,
His hands and cuffs ticking. We shall see
This moment repeated, years later
On television, when the astronauts
Train their camera back on us
As their ship pulls between Earth and the Moon.
Until we blink, there is nothing
In our lives to hold on to but
This honest perfection,
No response against perfect timing
Except to marvel, to tap along.

Photo of Miles Davis at Lennies-on-the-Turnpike, 1968

New York grows
Slimmer
In his absence.
I suppose

You could also title this picture
Of Miles, his leathery
Squint, the grace
In his fingers *a sliver of the stuff*

You can't get anymore,
As the rest of us wonder:
What was the name
Of the driver

Of that truck? And the rest
Of us sigh:
Death is one hell
Of a pickpocket.

Photo Of Dexter Gordon, About to Solo, 1965

To get the drift of this photo,
Think of the relationship between the sax
And the player's mouth as two halves
Of an exclamation point! What I mean is

Tonight, Dex means business. Ear mischief.
Let's–tear–DOWN–the–house–and–nobody
(ha!)–forced–you–(ha!)–to–come–here,
DID they? Think of a warrior's
Narrow sense of duty if you want to envision

His dark suit, or the way a pool hustler
Chalks his cue to understand the way Dex's
Fingers adjust his mouthpiece. What I mean is,
Dexter Gordon's about to take that DEEP breath,

The kind Superman took when he was too lazy
To waste muscle on the bad guys. A shock of wind,
A *what hit us?* And he could pick them up
Whenever he'd choose.

Photo of Milt Jackson, 1964

Mr. Jackson,
A young, black speechifier with an
I-Am-Serious! haircut
Pauses before his next number.
It is a portrait of vibeology,
A measurement of the soft vowels
And consonants a man must coax
From his mallets. And O, what will ring

From these spotlit bones?

Photo of Eric Dolphy, 1960

Here is a ballad
Within a ballad.
See how the stage lights
Diffuse about his head.

It is a portrait
Of a grace note.
The pause before
A conversation
Pulls down

To confidential
Breath.

And then, there are his eyes:
The distance they have journeyed,
The miraculous speech of the witness.

Chuck Berry

Hamburger wizard,
Loose-limbed instigator,
V-8 engine, purring for a storm

The evidence of a tight skirt, viewed from
    the window of a moving city bus,
Yelling her name, a spell, into the glass.
The amazing leap, from nobody to stockholder,
(*Look, Ma, no hands*), piped through a hot amp.

Figure skater on the rim of the invisible class wall,
The strength of the dreamer who wakes up, and it's
    Monday, a week of work, but gets out of bed

The unsung desire of the check-out clerk.
The shops of the sleepy backwater town,
    waiting for the kid to make good,
    to chauffeur home

The twang of the New Jersey turnpike
    in the wee, wee hours.
The myth of the lover as he passes, blameless,
    through the walls.

The fury hidden in the word *almost*.
The fury hidden in the word *please*.

The dream of one's name in lights,
Of sending the posse on the wrong trail,
Shaking the wounded Indian's hand, a brother.

The pulse of a crowd, knowing that the police
Have pushed in the door, dancing regardless

The frenzy of the word *go*.
The frenzy of the word *go*.
The frenzy of the word *go*.

The spark between the thought of the kiss
  and receiving the kiss,
The tension in these words:
  You Can't Dance.

The amazing duck walk.
The understanding that all it's going to take
  is one fast song.

The triumph in these words:
  Bye-bye, New Jersey, as if rising
  from a shallow grave.

The soda-jerk who plots doo-wop songs,
The well-intentioned Business School student
  who does what she's told, suspects
  they're keeping it hid.

Mr. Rock-n-Roll-jump-over
  (or get left behind),
Mr. *Taxes? Who, me?* Money beat,
Money beat, you can't catch me,
  (but they do),

A perpetual well of quarters in the pocket.
The incalculable hit of energy in the voice
  of a 16-year-old as her favorite band
  hits the stage,

And 10,000 pair of eyes look for what they're after:
  More.
And 10,000 voices roar for it:
  More.

And a multitude you wouldn't care to count
  surrounds the joint, waits for their opportunity
  to break in.

4: Small Moments

Youngblood

I'm sitting in a restaurant, having a very serious discussion on an eastern religion with my niece, when suddenly, out of the corner of my eye, I notice the way a young woman crosses the street.

Oh, look at the way she walks as she tries on for size what appears to be a new hairdo for her, a white woman with dreadlocks. She's announcing the changes to a friend who sits waiting for her on a trash can.

And she stops just before she reaches the curb, bends her head low like a wild mare and shakes her new look, tossing the braids aloft like strange, intelligent rope.

How like the woman I used to read about in Richard Brautigan's books, the young spirit with the power to postpone a man from whatever he was thinking, urge him to wipe his glasses to get a closer look.

I'm thinking of him right now, as this woman speaks young we're-hanging-out-on-a-summer's-afternoon things to her girl friend, and they cross back, leaving the afternoon alert and softly wobbling on its axis.

Tramp

I need a haircut, but this guy clearly doesn't understand what's on my head. I become nervous when I see a blank stare as I try to explain to him what a slow fade is.

What can I say about the history of my hair? Once, I had a poetry manuscript which had the word *nappy* mixed somewhere in its title; once, I wore different floppy hats; once, you could set my blood to boil simply by pulling an afro pick from out of a back pocket, rake a soft "do" as if God played fashion favorites.

In high school in the late sixties, weren't our afros mythical? Didn't George Jackson die because some guards believed his hair was capable of storage, little bush of anger, tiny grove of long, hidden blades?

How many times did my family think a proper haircut would put my feet on the right path, set my mind straight? Once, my father got a cousin who was a back-alley barber to "relax" my hair. When he was finished with the uneven lye, and before he cut it, I was able to look in a shard of mirror, see that my hair happened to be longer than my mother's, all that wound-up energy given permission to roll, to blow in a breeze.

I was so pissed-off by this "cure" that I let it go to hell, let it tangle into long, vengeful dreads I wasn't to cut until I began teaching college, and only then because the school was down south.

Some friends innocently recommended this new hair place, just a few blocks from my house. The barber's friendly and game, but he's up against home-boy hair, urban steel wool, industrial-strength kink.

We both act as if we're on a bad blind date, well-intentioned, but soon forgotten. I leave forty dollars lighter, a few snips cleaner, and carrying a memory of one of my dear aunts, who didn't know what to make of this mess either.

Cornbread

for Charles Simic

After the reading, at the reception, the famous poet
surrounded by the aftermath of his brilliance, the female
poetry editor and struggling novelist both swooning over
the hidden lust in his voice, a star cornered by outstretched
volumes of his works and pen-points, and on the table,
cornbread.

Sweet, sweet cornbread! Deep flavor of my childhood and
my mother's wax paper. Delicious cornbread, last thing in
the world I was thinking of, last item I'd expect to see lying
around in a cookie tin, the air abuzz with abstraction and
praise's light meters.

Charlie Chaplin Impersonates a Poet

The stage is set for imminent disaster.
Here is the little tramp, standing
On a stack of books in order
To reach the microphone, the
Poet he's impersonating somehow
Trussed and mumbling in a
Tweed bundle at his feet.

He opens his mouth: *Tra-la!*
Out comes doves, incandescent bulbs,
Plastic roses. *Well, that's that,*
Squirms the young professor who's
Coordinated this,
No more visiting poets!

His department head groans
For the trap door. As it
Swings away

The tramp keeps on as if
Nothing has occurred,
A free arm mimicking
A wing.

A Small Moment

I walk into the bakery next door
To my apartment. They are about
To pull some sort of toast with cheese
From the oven. When I ask:
What's that smell? I am being
A poet, I am asking

What everyone else in the shop
Wanted to ask, but somehow couldn't;
I am speaking on behalf of two other
Customers who wanted to buy the
Name of it. I ask the woman
Behind the counter for a percentage
Of her sale. Am I flirting?
Am I happy because the days
Are longer? Here's what

She does: She takes her time
Choosing the slices. "I am picking
Out the good ones," she tells me. It's
April 14th. Spring, with five to ten
Degrees to go. Some days, I feel my duty;
Some days, I love my work.

Walt Whitman Mall

Wouldn't it have been wonderful, if on his deathbed,
The world of literature had opened up for poor
   Walt Whitman,
Poor white beard,
The future guessed, but too slow
To do him any good.

This is the drawback with clairvoyance,
If you have the misfortune
To imagine a future
Only a part of you will inhabit.
What would it have hurt to let the old duffer
Know

A few of his hunches were on the money.
Wouldn't it have been the height of kindness
If, on the way out,
Some force—an angel, say, or a muse,
Pulled a bit of mischief
In the name of what-does-it-matter
And sloppy American genius,

Showed Walt a few seconds of evidence
—say, a teenaged boy, seeking out
          his book in a mall,
—say, the religion of commerce
          and distribution,
And his name lit up on the highway.

The Death of Sam Patch

"There's no mistake in Sam Patch!"
—his last words

No, there's no mistaking Mr. Patch.
History will lead him to a watery grave
In my home town of Rochester, NY.
He will disappear after he jumps
Only to return with the spring thaw.
There is so much in his brief fame
To ponder, that tugs at us.
Rochester, like any milltown,
Is full of reckless death,
Yet the fate of Patch was on a par
With the local Native Americans, at least
When I attended grade school:
We were taught the story
Of a man who made his living
Oddly, with a tame black bear
And calculation.
Any school child my age
Recalls his last moments on Earth.
—Was there actually
A parade? A premonition?
Did he really waver at the top of the platform
Just before he jumped? Any contemporary of mine
Carries this, the language his body,
A wrong angle, recites
As it hits the gorge.
Here is the regret of the
Tightrope walker, and of course,
A kid's morbid curiosity
—A body, suspended in ice,
Worked over three months
By the elements
—What happens? One can only guess

How far away it must have seemed
From the energy of his last words,
No mistake in the way he brandished them
Against the spray.
William Carlos Williams
Will make much of the beginnings
Of our Icarus,
Who gets his start in Patterson, NJ,
To plunge headlong into my town's
Settler past. What else have I learned
Besides the beauty of the dare?

I'll Fly Away

O, young black American teenaged boychild, I
know what runs through your head
        In Venice at the bridge at Accademia. A bit of
lire has slipped from your pocket,
        A young white foreign woman has seen this,
picks it up, and calls
        For your attention. Your cautious response
is more than a difference of tongues.
        Your body tenses; a traditional brace
for the blues.

        She is smiling and tries to hand
your money back. A bit of you is
        still back in the States,
Where a simple exchange like this
        sometimes hides a stiff reminder.
Clearly, my brother, this isn't the world

        We come from. In mid-day Venice
You move towards her outstretched arm
        a little slower than shy,
As if you'll have need of a sober witness,
        as if this is where you know
The experiment ends, and memory dogs
        'round the corner.

Eye Sight to the Blind

It was early afternoon. The light slanted through the window of the train my wife and I were traveling on from Venice to Lake Como.

I am not known as a romantic poet, a fact my wife has brought to my fuzzy attention more than once.

But though I have known this woman for most of my adult life, I had never seen her quite like this.

The light had caught my wife and for a brief moment it seemed as if every gram of her essence, all the elements that have cleaved me to her were broadcast into the forced air of the compartment.

Everybody fightin' about it, goes the old song, and, Good God, I understood why. *She is so lovely*, thought my beggar's eyes, *and I'm allowed to belong to all that.*

Little Red Rooster

At the dinner table the night before we left Italy, a man told us a story of accidentally looking up while hiking to see the face of a red-headed woman, haloed by the sunlight.

How would the blues treat this moment of his epiphany?

Like a sweaty moment during the service.

Like a minister getting down to the good stuff and rolling up his sleeves.

Like the good sisters getting ready to let go in the amen corner.

And how beautiful was this woman, that he sees only for a moment?

I thought of my father's term for it, could almost hear his appraisal as he speaks. *That woman*, my daddy would have said, *was a popper-stopper.*

After that afternoon, the man tells us, he could almost believe in the concept of God. *Do you believe?* he would ask my wife, *do you believe in God?* Beneath his question, the hounds began to howl.

Hard Times

And this is for Etheridge, whom I never met, but feel a certain kinship with. We share a long distance story, a kind of bond by blue coincidence.

A few years before his death, he was homeless in New York and living in a city shelter. He had just finished teaching a workshop at the 63rd St. Y about the time I was teaching there, and somehow, someone from the *Voice* found out, tracked him down, and wrote a feature on him.

When the article appeared weeks later, there was a head shot of Etheridge. *Hard Times* was the caption.

How many of our songs are fleshed with what he had to say? It was *Nobody Knows You When You're Down and Out*. It was *Rollin' and Tumblin'*. It was *You Can't Lose What You Ain't Never Had*, but he was still willing to double-cross the trickster, still smiling and laughing about dancing.

Roll on, Etheridge, roll on. He and I look nothing alike, but our tongues do what they must, and our skin's that dark river Langston writes of, and for months after that article ran, people'd walk up to me with that barely hidden, amazed-you're-still-walking-the-face-of-the-earth expression on their face and ask: *Didn't I read something about you in the Voice?*

And these days, I lie and say *yeah*, but I'm not lying, even though I'll never be king of the dozens.

CARNEGIE MELLON POETRY

1975
The Living and the Dead, Ann Hayes
In the Face of Descent, T. Alan Broughton

1976
The Week the Dirigible Came, Jay Meek
Full of Lust and Good Usage, Stephen Dunn

1977
How I Escaped from the Labyrinth and Other Poems, Philip Dacey
The Lady from the Dark Green Hills, Jim Hall
For Luck: Poems 1962-1977, H.L. Van Brunt
By the Wreckmaster's Cottage, Paula Rankin

1978
New & Selected Poems, James Bertolino
The Sun Fetcher, Michael Dennis Browne
A Circus of Needs, Stephen Dunn
The Crowd Inside, Elizabeth Libbey

1979
Paying Back the Sea, Philip Dow
Swimmer in the Rain, Robert Wallace
Far from Home, T. Alan Broughton
The Room Where Summer Ends, Peter Cooley
No Ordinary World, Mekeel McBride

1980
And the Man Who Was Traveling Never Got Home, H.L. Van Brunt
Drawing on the Walls, Jay Meek
The Yellow House on the Corner, Rita Dove
The 8-Step Grapevine, Dara Wier
The Mating Reflex, Jim Hall

1981
A Little Faith, John Skoyles
Augers, Paula Rankin
Walking Home from the Icehouse, Vern Rutsala
Work and Love, Stephen Dunn
The Rote Walker, Mark Jarman
Morocco Journal, Richard Harteis
Songs of a Returning Soul, Elizabeth Libbey

1982
The Granary, Kim R. Stafford
Calling the Dead, C.G. Hanzlicek
Dreams Before Sleep, T. Alan Broughton
Sorting It Out, Anne S. Perlman
Love Is Not a Consolation; It Is a Light, Primus St. John

1983
The Going Under of the Evening Land, Mekeel McBride

Museum, Rita Dove
Air and Salt, Eve Shelnutt
Nightseasons, Peter Cooley

1984

Falling from Stardom, Jonathan Holden
Miracle Mile, Ed Ochester
Girlfriends and Wives, Robert Wallace
Earthly Purposes, Jay Meek
Not Dancing, Stephen Dunn
The Man in the Middle, Gregory Djanikian
A Heart Out of This World, David James
All You Have in Common, Dara Wier

1985

Smoke from the Fires, Michael Dennis Browne
Full of Lust and Good Usage, Stephen Dunn (2nd edition)
Far and Away, Mark Jarman
Anniversary of the Air, Michael Waters
To the House Ghost, Paula Rankin
Midwinter Transport, Anne Bromley

1986

Seals in the Inner Harbor, Brendan Galvin
Thomas and Beulah, Rita Dove
Further Adventures With You, C.D. Wright
Fifteen to Infinity, Ruth Fainlight
False Statements, Jim Hall
When There Are No Secrets, C.G. Hanzlicek

1987

Some Gangster Pain, Gillian Conoley
Other Children, Lawrence Raab
Internal Geography, Richard Harteis
The Van Gogh Notebook, Peter Cooley
A Circus of Needs, Stephen Dunn (2nd edition)
Ruined Cities, Vern Rutsala
Places and Stories, Kim R. Stafford

1988

Preparing to Be Happy, T. Alan Broughton
Red Letter Days, Mekeel McBride
The Abandoned Country, Thomas Rabbitt
The Book of Knowledge, Dara Wier
Changing the Name to Ochester, Ed Ochester
Weaving the Sheets, Judith Root

1989

Recital in a Private Home, Eve Shelnutt
A Walled Garden, Michael Cuddihy
The Age of Krypton, Carol J. Pierman
Land That Wasn't Ours, David Keller

Stations, Jay Meek
The Common Summer: New and Selected Poems, Robert Wallace
The Burden Lifters, Michael Waters
Falling Deeply into America, Gregory Djanikian
Entry in an Unknown Hand, Franz Wright

1990

Why the River Disappears, Marcia Southwick
Staying Up For Love, Leslie Adrienne Miller
Dreamer, Primus St. John

1991

Permanent Change, John Skoyles
Clackamas, Gary Gildner
Tall Stranger, Gillian Conoley
The Gathering of My Name, Cornelius Eady
A Dog in the Lifeboat, Joyce Peseroff
Raised Underground, Renate Wood
Divorce: A Romance, Paula Rankin

1992

Modern Ocean, James Harms
The Astonished Hours, Peter Cooley
You Won't Remember This, Michael Dennis Browne
Twenty Colors, Elizabeth Kirschner
First A Long Hesitation, Eve Shelnutt
Bountiful, Michael Waters
Blue for the Plough, Dara Wier
All That Heat in a Cold Sky, Elizabeth Libbey

1993

Trumpeter, Jeannine Savard
Cuba, Ricardo Pau-Llosa
The Night World and the Word Night, Franz Wright
The Book of Complaints, Richard Katrovas

1994

If Winter Come: Collected Poems, 1967–1992, Alvin Aubert
Of Desire and Disorder, Wayne Dodd
Ungodliness, Leslie Adrienne Miller
Rain, Henry Carlile
Windows, Jay Meek
A Handful of Bees, Dzvinia Orlowsky

1995

Germany, Caroline Finkelstein
Housekeeping in a Dream, Laura Kasischke
About Distance, Gregory Djanikian
Wind of the White Dresses, Mekeel McBride
Above the Tree Line, Kathy Mangan
In the Country of Elegies, T. Alan Broughton

Scenes from the Light Years, Anne C. Bromley
Quartet, Angela Ball

1996
Back Roads, Patricia Henley
Dyer's Thistle, Peter Balakian
Beckon, Gillian Conoley
The Parable of Fire, James Reiss
Cold Pluto, Mary Ruefle
Orders of Affection, Arthur Smith
Colander, Michael McFee

1997
Growing Darkness, Growing Light, Jean Valentine
Selected Poems, 1965-1995, Michael Dennis Browne
Your Rightful Childhood: New and Selected Poems, Paula Rankin
Headlands: New and Selected Poems, Jay Meek
Soul Train, Allison Joseph
Autobiography of a Jukebox, Cornelius Eady
The Patience of the Cloud Photographer, Elizabeth Holmes
Madly in Love, Aliki Barnstone